Dear Jia,

Six Secrets for Parents to Help Their Kids Achieve in School

Meline M. Kevorkian, Ed.D.

Parents are the first and most important teachers!

Best wishes,

Meline Kevorkian

ScarecrowEducation
Lanham, Maryland • Toronto • Oxford
2005

Published in the United States of America
by ScarecrowEducation
An imprint of The Rowman & Littlefield Publishing Group, Inc.
4501 Forbes Boulevard, Suite 200, Lanham, Maryland 20706
www.scarecroweducation.com

PO Box 317
Oxford
OX2 9RU, UK

British Library Cataloguing in Publication Information Available

Library of Congress Cataloging-in-Publication Data

Kevorkian, Meline M., 1968–
  Six secrets for parents to help their kids achieve in school / Meline M.
Kevorkian.
    p. cm.
  Includes bibliographical references.
  ISBN 1-57886-239-6 (pbk. : alk. paper)
  1. Education, Elementary—Parent participation. 2. Academic
achievement. I. Title.

LB1048.5.K48 2005
371.19'2—dc22
                                                    2004026698

To my greatest teachers,
my mom and dad,
for making me all that I am,
loving me all that they can,
supporting me all the way,
and always making me smile on a rainy day.
Thank you,
Moug

Contents

Introduction

Rush, rush, go, go, to the never-ending errands, appointments, and over-whelming schedules we are all caught up in. We dream of summer and a break from the stress of school days. No matter what we do, we never seen to feel that it is enough to make our children soar in school and gain a strong educational foundation. Sadly, there is no escape and no magic potion to quiet our busy and bustling lifestyles, but there are many se-crets to ease the pressure and the tension in our lives as parents.

We have the great responsibility to make sure our children's needs are taken care of, from doctor appointments to meal preparation to school, homework, sports, and social activities. Of course, that is just the beginning; we also must take time to love and praise our kids and plan all the things that we need to do together and share together as families. Wow, it's a tough road, but a rewarding one, and we are all in it together.

Unfortunately, as hard as we try to balance this spinning ball, we can easily lose sight of our original goals. Sometimes we must take a step back and really take a good look to assess our lifestyles and situations that surround us, to make an appropriate evaluation of our priorities, and to see that they all are in the right order. This is something we, as parents, have to do to keep our children on the right path for their suc-cessful futures.

Perhaps we are paying too much attention to one aspect of our chil-dren's development, when in reality, our attention should be on some-thing else in their lives. Spending our time and theirs on the proper pri-orities isn't easy, but it can be done, no matter where the child attends school and no matter who the parent is or what his or her educational level may be. It is all about priorities and organizing time to meet them.

Family time, open communication, school, studies, and of course children's basic needs are paramount, and that is why I have written this simple and comprehensible book of six secrets that you can use right now. A little advice in the right direction can go a long way. As a working mother and educator, I feel driven to reach every family and child, to help them help themselves to get a good education and realize their goals and dreams.

I was raised in a close-knit family, and on most days, my mother spent her afternoons tending to my two live-in grandmothers, my father, my sister, my brother, and me. She did all this in addition to working with my dad in the family business. At 2:30, when the school bell rang and her paid workday ended, the fun began. Her duties included soccer practice, allergy shots, picking up grandma's arthritis medicine, taking the dog to the vet, grocery shopping, school projects, homework, dinner, baths, and laundry. She did all this with a smile on her face and, to my childish eyes, what appeared to be very little effort. I remember my mom and dad never seemed to relax, but they always found the time to inquire about school with daily questions about what we learned and where we were going. I guess it's safe to say it is not luck that my sister, brother, and I graduated with honors from college.

My parents frequently remind me how easy parenting is today, compared to when I was a child. I remember them running around and always being busy, but I also remember the hugs, the quiet times, the school projects, the metaphorical Band Aids, and the little games to help me prepare for tests and the rhymes to remember history facts. My parents cared about my education and me, and it still shows in me today. What inspired me the most was how they balanced three kids and their different interests. My sister, the roller skater, my brother, the disco king, and me, the horseback rider, were nurtured to always be our best, to love learning, life, and each other.

No matter what our circumstances or backgrounds are, as parents, we are alike in many ways. From the moment our little blessings were placed in our arms, we felt great love, pride, thankfulness, and an overwhelming sense of responsibility. At first, it is just basic care consisting of love, nourishment, and lots of cleaning. Then, within the blink of an eye, the reality of a child's care and his or her future sets in, and we, as parents, know the number one priority is, of course, education. For successful results, it takes hard work on our part and our children's, but the good news is that it can be done and it can be enjoyable for you and them. It really is not about the school your child attends; rather it is about *how you and your child attend school.* When you, your child, and your child's teachers work together to put your student's best foot forward, you have a winning combination.

Comparing is part of everyday life, especially when it comes to decisions for our children; we compare schools, teachers, clubs, teams, scores, and other children. Standardized tests describe our children as average, above average, or below average, and too often we assume these tests are predictors of long-term success. Private schools have been very successful at helping children achieve regardless of where they start, and this success has been looked at but never "bottled and sold." I would like to share the recipe with you. The special formula can and should be used by parents to make a big difference in their children's academic lives, regardless of where they go to school.

Children spend the majority of their childhoods in school, and having children succeed in school is every parent's wish. It is very easy for parents to become frustrated and have a feeling of being helpless when their children do not do well. You are not alone! Private tutoring and evaluation services are often very expensive, and sometimes, once their services are completed, children fall back into the same patterns that brought them there to begin with.

A child's education today is no longer a luxury available to an exclusive group of people, but a necessity for all. Children must be educated to higher levels and learn more sophisticated skills that will carry them to higher education and the future workforce. Parents, along with the schools, can provide the best opportunity for true learning and success in school. All parents, regardless of their own educational levels, can have an impact on their children's learning and help them reach their potential. There are no acceptable reasons or excuses for not making your home a center for learning; your commitment as a parent is to require learning and to produce children eager to learn.

Since 1990, I have been both a teacher and an administrator in public and private schools. I have had firsthand experience with almost every type of struggle parents have faced with their children in regard to school. I have seen very bright children be unsuccessful at school and average children achieve beyond belief. I began a collection of the characteristics shared by successful students and their parents. For many years, I continually thought about all the "tricks" that help children achieve, and I realized that many of them were easy to carry out but far too often not utilized.

As an administrator in a private school, I rarely make it through a day without an abundance of conferences, both over the phone and in person. These conferences shed light on how specific parenting beliefs and involvement significantly affect a child's academic life. It was after many of these meetings that I concluded parents need to realize that they can make a difference, and it is as easy as reading about and implementing six secrets.

Schools should be thought of not only as places for students, but also as places for families. Many educators are discouraged by the illusion that parents lack interest in their children's education. Parents want children to excel and want to be involved; however, sometimes they do not know how, or where, to begin. Even the busiest of parents have the ability to be involved and influence the educational development of their children.

Having children enjoy learning and allowing them the experience of accomplishment may be easier than you ever imagined. This book has six easy secrets to guide parents, like you, in making the best choices to help their children reach their academic potential and goals, without pressure or pain. The first section in each chapter, "Real Stories and Fears," is filled with stories of real parents and the fears they have had about their children's education and their parenting skills. In the second section, "Secret for Success," you will find easy advice to help you give your child every advantage, regardless of his or her school. The third section, "Gaining the Private School Edge," is a quick summary of advice and tips to assist your child.

Educational Values, High Expectations, and Goals

This chapter contains four real-life situations in which parents have questioned their actions or lack of action. Although we know it's wrong, we all, at times, compare our children to other kids of similar age. Why do we do this? It's easy; we all want the best for our own children. When our children are sad, we're sad; when they're ill, we feel sick. But when they're not living up to their potential, we feel lost and sometimes helpless. It is okay and normal; parental love will do that to you.

The good news is that you can fix all this just by expanding this tremendous love. Loving isn't enough; you must be their mentor, their psychologist, their disciplinarian, their friend, and their best critic. When we push hard, let them believe it's a gentle shove. When we correct, let them believe it's just good advice, and whatever it takes for them to succeed, let them know they can do it and will do it and you'll always be by their side. Reading this book will help you to help them, and all our futures will be brighter.

REAL STORIES AND FEARS

The Neighbor's Son, Age 9

Your neighbors show you their child's report card. All As, great comments, and a honor roll seal. Their son goes to a private school. He reads in his spare time, and when you talk with him, you begin to wonder why your child is not as articulate and struggles when reading stories. Have you ever worried that you are not doing enough with your child, and is the school doing enough? Is there a problem with your child? Why does the child on the block who attends private school remember all his books and know how to do his homework? What makes him so motivated? Is it the school, the child, the home life, or genetics? Is it too late to help, and what do I do?

Lori, Age 6

Lori, a little girl on your child's gymnastic team, talks to you after every practice. She tells about her school day and all the interesting things she learned. When you ask your child about her school day, she responds with, "I don't know" or "I can't remember" or just the word "good." Lori and your daughter went to the same preschool, but she went to a private elementary school for kindergarten. Why doesn't your own daughter discuss her school day with you? Is it her, is it you, or does she just feel you're not interested? Does she like school? Are the teachers capturing her attention?

Karen, Age 8

Karen reads all the time. You see her sitting at the ballpark reading while her brother plays ball. When you sit near her, she tells you about the book she read last week and her favorite part. Karen goes to a parochial school. You can barely get your child to read what is required for school. She cries and carries on and says she doesn't understand anything when you ask her questions. Maybe she's not interested enough; perhaps she doesn't realize the importance or learning. You wonder, what can you do to turn this problem around?

Brian, Age 11

Brian knows exactly what he wants to be, the college he wants to attend, and just what he has to do to make his dreams come true. He talks about his future and how hard he is trying for honor roll. School is on his mind, and it shows. He knows about grade point averages and college requirements and how they will affect his future. Brian goes to an all boys prep school. It is clear that Brian's family is totally involved with him and his goals. Is it too late for you to stress the importance of a good education to your child?

SECRET FOR SUCCESS #1: HAVE HIGH EXPECTATIONS, MODEL STRONG EDUCATIONAL VALUES, AND ENCOURAGE GOAL SETTING AND BIG DREAMS!

For any organization to succeed there needs to be a shared vision, so every member knows what the goals are, what needs to be accomplished, and what contribution is expected of him. A family unit works in that same way, encouraging each member to make goals and strive to make those goals a reality. As a parent, your belief that your child can, and should, flourish in school must be embedded in all you say and do so that he or she knows that learning and academic achievement are not optional.

Children who succeed know what is expected of them by their parents and what they need to do to meet those expectations. Parents are responsible for setting the ground rules and expectations for children and for providing them with a vision of success. Private schools have a clear, defined vision that is the selling point to the families they serve. Private school parents usually share a common commitment to academic success for their children. This vision is defined early on and made into a mission and philosophy, which are indoctrinated in the child. Children with a vision know where they are going and how they are going to get there. Expectations are high, and children are aware of their responsibilities intellectually and socially. Shortcomings are addressed readily. Consequences for inappropriate and nonproductive behavior are apparent and such behavior is dealt with appropriately, and the only option is improvement without excuses. The child learns and shares the vision of doing his or her best with parents, teachers, and the school.

Most successful students have a driving force and support system that stem from their homes, and when you talk with their parents, they usually know what their children are doing in school, what they are learning about, and what their children want to be. Ask yourself the following questions, and if you cannot answer many of them, do your homework: Do you know what your child is learning right now? Do you know if he finds it interesting? When is her next chapter exam? Do you know what her favorite subject is? Is he reading a book right now? What is his favorite book? What does she want to be when she grows up? Does he like his school? Teacher? Etc.? The first step to helping your child succeed in school is making learning the highest priority in your home. Your words and actions should demonstrate to your child that learning new information is pleasurable and important. Being knowledgeable gives you a feeling of confidence and reassurance of who you are.

Reading should be a habit you instill and practice. An abundance of research indicates that the amount of time a student spends on independent reading has a significant influence on how he or she will do in school and on standardized tests. Parents can improve their children's academic success by modeling and promoting reading in the home. Read yourself, and discuss things you are reading with your child. Share questions you have and the answers you find. Make it a point to look up places and events that interest you and tell your children about them. Spark a curiosity for the world around them. Turn off the television!

Ideally, children should be read to from earliest childhood. Listening to good and interesting literature will turn them on to reading. As they grow and enter school, you can introduce age-appropriate books so they may begin reading some of the words. Start slow so you don't overwhelm or frustrate them, and increase the amount they read as their skills improve. Have them point to the words as they read them to keep their place.

There are many simple, commonly used words called "sight words" that should be reviewed. Obtain a list from your child's school. It is never too early to promote reading comprehension. Ask your child questions about the story or book. Keep in mind the five Ws: who, what, when, where, and why. Discuss her favorite part. With older children, follow the saying "better late than never" and begin a regular routine of reading. Have a designated minilibrary in your home. Older children may read independently while others family members do so simultaneously. Remember, to encourage daily reading, you must read and practice what you preach. As Albert Einstein said, "If you want your children to be brilliant, read them fairy tales. If you want them to be more brilliant, read them more fairy tales." Books and newspapers should be as or more important than television and radio. Children tend to value what parents do. So show your children you value books, learning, and school.

Don't ever underestimate the parental responsibility of instilling the power and love of reading. You would never think about not giving nourishment to your child's body, so don't neglect his mind. Children have a great ability to repeat and remember things that we may not want them to. At some point, we have experienced or heard a story about something a child said that shocked or embarrassed the parent. Make certain that when it comes to their school and teachers, everything "out of the mouths of babes" is positive, interesting, and encouraging.

When you have concerns about your child's teachers or school, address them with the proper authorities, and never let the child hear you be negative. Speak of your child's teachers and administrators as respected sources of knowledge and guidance and your children are likely to follow.

When your child enters school or a new class, clearly define your expectations. Children generally want to please their parents, so accept nothing but their best. The most important rule in regard to school should be that each child works to his or her highest potential. Instill learning when they are young and it should stay with them throughout their lives. Be a source of encouragement. Tell them that they can accomplish anything they set their minds to. When you believe in yourself and others support you, the sky is the limit. Being knowledgeable gives children great confidence and prepares them for life's journey ahead.

Set goals directly related to school, such as completed homework assignments. Set aside daily study time, and do not accept excuses for low performance. Children should be taught early that a good solid education can make their goals a reality. When children strive to improve themselves, focusing on subjects that they are particularly weak in, all things become possible. This is especially true when it comes to school and learning. Persuade your children to try harder, rather than nagging them to bring home good grades. Make them understand that rarely does anything come easily. Tell them that learning is hard work and should be taken seriously, but also that it can be really fun and rewarding. If help is needed, get it for them. Children should be reminded that "doing your best" is more than just a worn-out phrase. It should be a goal set by children and expected by parents. Some children may need help or hints in identifying their dreams; set aside the time. Then discuss what they need to do to accomplish these dreams. Reward your children's efforts, not just their achievements.

Often, our children can do better. What can parents do to help? Try raising the bar by setting high standards and expectations. Don't accept mediocrity if your child is capable of excellence. Let your child feel it is just a nudge, but you know it's really a push, and when the results are good, celebrate with them. Remember, children need our help to succeed. Your child's best efforts may not be perfect, but that's okay. Children who know that someone believes in them are motivated to do much more. We, as parents, must define the work ethic we expect from them. We must believe our children should learn to put forth their best effort. Fortunately, many students believe their effort directly affects school achievement and most want to do well. Fear of failure sometimes overwhelms them and keeps them from attaining higher achievements. They don't want to try due to this fear. We must remind them that occasional failure is a part of life, but stamina, determination, and effort will always prevail and will pay off in the long run.

Students who study too little learn too little, and parents play an important role in encouraging study habits and effort level. Expect the best, believe in their ability, and value their education and learning. To raise a child who believes in himself is to raise a winner.

Children model the behavior of parents. Teach children to listen by being a good listener. When you speak, expect the same courtesy. Listening is a skill that must be learned and practiced, just as being respectful and courteous. Talking to our children as we would our friends invites our youngsters to seek us out as confidants. When they talk, stop what you are doing and give them your undivided attention. Let the child know that you are interested, understanding, involved, and available. Make the effort to listen carefully, as interrupting and interjecting comments will make them hesitant to talk. Always encourage them to share what they are doing and be eager to assist them in any way. Open your child's curiosity whenever possible. This stirs her interest to discover the world around her. Help them want to study by reminding them that the word *study* means "learn about," and it helps make us knowledgeable and interesting.

GAINING THE PRIVATE SCHOOL EDGE: PRACTICAL EXAMPLES, AND GUIDES TO GET YOU STARTED

Tip #1: Make learning the highest priority. Help make learning an enjoyable pastime.

Maria, Mother

Maria has her daughter Susanna's friend over to play. Maria admires Susanna's friend's choice of vocabulary and ability to discuss many topics. Maria wonders why Susanna doesn't have the same ability to talk about creative and interesting things. Maria is unaware that Susanna's friend has parents who find "everyday" activities to spark curiosity and to engage her in learning. Cooking is used as an avenue to engage in math, measurement, and following directions. Trips to the library and bookstore are commonplace. Everyone reads, and family discussions are frequent.

Advice for Getting Susanna on the Right Track

Susanna should be exposed to places that create a longing for learning, such as children's museums, reading circles at bookstores or libraries, and other fun family activities that open young minds. Children can and should be included in everyday activities and given opportunities to participate, question, and experience.

Your Current Situation: Where Are You Now?

Ask yourself these questions and reflect on the answers:

- Does your child know where to do homework?
- Does your child ask you for help when he is having difficulty?
- Do you know your child's favorite subject?
- Do you know her areas of strength and weakness?
- Does your child know what your expectations are for his academic achievement?
- Does your child have goals for school and learning?
- Do you praise your child for accomplishments and efforts is school?

- Do you know what your child may want to be or pursue in the future?
- Do you have a home library?
- Do you look for ways to involve your child and spark her curiosity?

Tip #2: Expect their best; don't accept anything less than their best effort. Set high expectations. Believe in their ability and help them recognize their capabilities. Discuss their dreams. Set goals.

Thomas, Age 10

Thomas doesn't always complete his homework. His grades and test scores reflect this behavior. When his mom comes home from work, she always asks if his homework is done. Thomas usually says he is done or nods his head. He usually forgets to do something or leaves the book or paper in school. Thomas's mom cares about school and inquires but does not set clear expectations and goals with Thomas for his homework. She accepts his word and chooses not to see for herself what the homework is and if it is completed.

Advice for Getting Thomas on the Right Track

Thomas should have a planner or notebook in which he writes down his assignments and the materials he needs to take home. This should be used as a guide when packing his backpack at the end of the day. His parent should check it daily and be sure he completes all assignments. Over time, writing down assignments, bringing home his materials, and completing assignments will become part of his daily routine.

Create a list of expectations and goals and chart your child's progress.

When we start a job we are usually given a list of responsibilities and expectations, as well as policies and procedures, to help us accomplish our duties. Children need nurturing, love, support, and our guiding hand. Make your directions and expectations clear. Write your expectations down and have your children set goals to reach them. They will respond! Never hesitate to spot check, review, or discuss homework on a regular basis. A few minutes a day may make the difference.

Describe the current practice in your home.

Example: He comes everyday and knows he must do his homework before anything else.

_____
_____
_____
_____

Your Expectations: The ideal situation.

Example: Do your homework everyday and be prepared for school.

_____
_____
_____

Reaching the Goal: Using the current practice as a baseline and the expectation, set goals together.

Example: I will turn in my homework everyday and seek help when I don't understand something.

_____
_____
_____

Make It a Priority: Be there to follow up on all rules; Show your child he is your top priority.

Example: Homework will be done before television, talking on the phone, or using the computer or Internet.

_____
_____
_____

Chart the Progress and Praise Effort and Accomplishment:

Example:

Date	Homework		Completed
Monday	Yes	No	
Tuesday	Yes	No	
Wednesday	Yes	No	
Thursday	Yes	No	
Friday	Yes	No	

Reward: All-week success = Trip to the bookstore or library.

CHAPTER 2

Your Child's Perceptions of Self

Most students in private school are aware of how important asking questions is, along with teacher relationships, especially if they don't fully understand something. One afternoon, Johnny came home from public school with a homework assignment and did not understand anything he was supposed to do. His mother asked repeatedly, "Why didn't you ask the teacher for help?" He replied, "She is too busy; she gets mad when we ask questions; she doesn't like me!" The family atmosphere fostered in many private schools makes asking questions and requesting clarifying information a comfort zone. You too can create a comfort zone for your child and give your child the confidence to approach his teachers.

You are driving to pick your son up from school thinking of all the things you have to do when you get home. As he enters the car, you begin to vent your disappointment with the way he left his room and the bathroom when he left for school. You start the lecture by letting him know what you expect and how unacceptable the state of the house was and that you are not a slave and don't understand how you have raised such a sloppy person. Little do you know he had a rough day himself. Math class was hard, he was frustrated, his friends ignored him most of the day, and at lunch they hid his lunchbox. The last thing he needs is to be picked on by his mother. He wonders why you couldn't remember how he helped clean up last night and took out the garbage. He begins to feel that no matter what he does or doesn't do, you will always find something to be upset at and that he is incapable of pleasing you. He decides not to share the grade he got on his math quiz even though he would like you to help him with it.

Sometimes, without realizing it, we set up a negative environment in our homes that causes our children to feel poorly about themselves and be reluctant to share their troubles, weaknesses, and difficulties. Your home should be a safe haven where they can bring their "problems" and feel all can be overcome and that tomorrow will be a new and better day and they'll be ready to tackle anything. Successful children have supportive parents who bring out their best. You have to feel your best to do your best. A child's perception of self is one of the most important issues in how well she achieves in life. When your child attends a function where he feels and looks fantastic, he will have a good time regardless of how the function was or wasn't. On the other hand, if he feels badly about how he looks or what he is wearing, he will have a terrible time at that very same function. This just reinforces the theory of self-perception; you must feel good to do good. The better we feel about ourselves, the better we do. Your child's perception of self will affect every aspect of her life, and you, the parent, play an integral part in building a strong self-perception for her. Most private schools are learning communities where every child is viewed as an important part of the "learning family," and embedded in the curriculum are core beliefs that build a child's self-esteem. Their capabilities are viewed as boundless and all children are capable and valuable. This belief is indoctrinated into the school through the rules, mission, curriculum, and teaching strategies. As a parent, your responsibility, regardless of your child's school, is to help your child realize her value, feel positive about her capabilities, and be praised and cherished by you.

REAL STORIES AND FEARS

Michael, Age 8

Michael comes home every Friday with his school papers and a worried look on his face. He knows that his mother will not be happy when she sees his grades. He studies really hard but never seems to be able to do well on tests. He gets in the car and says, "I'm sorry, Mom; I guess I'm just stupid." He wishes he could go to his cousin's school, a private religious school, because his cousin tells him that everyone does well there. His cousin says you aren't allowed to fail at his school.

Is it really the school or does it begin at home? Parents can bring out their children's best by fostering a belief in themselves.

Kimberly, Age 11

Kimberly goes to public school and often feels lost and overwhelmed. She would love to run for student council, but she feels that she would never make it because she doesn't know most of the kids and they don't know her. In private school there seems to be less of a chance of feeling "lost in a crowd." Teachers seem to "know" their students and encourage them to join clubs and extracurricular activities and get involved. Private school parents assist their children to find areas they can excel in to help them build their confidence. Parents must provide opportunities for accomplishment. Whether they make it isn't important; however, in the process they will make friends and gain confidence. Behind every successful student is a supportive parent.

Jessica, Age 10

Jessica refuses to try to answer difficult questions or participate in school activities. When the teacher asks her why she never raises her hand to answer a question, she responds, "I don't want to get it wrong." At school, if you say the wrong thing, the other children laugh, and the teacher lets them. If she could, she would never say a word at school. At home, she feels that everything she says is ridiculed. Her brother and sister make fun of her, and her parents let them. Whatever she does or says, her parents find it unacceptable; they scream at her. She's filled with negativity and prefers just to stay quiet and out of the way. This is the time to instill confidence and change something negative into something positive. Patience, kindness, respect, and understanding go a long way to fix the perceptions children have of themselves. You must treat your children the way you want to be treated.

Tatiana, Age 7

Tatiana gets sent to the principal's office on a regular basis. She is very talkative and immature and is constantly disrupting her classmates.

When asked why she doesn't follow the rules or listen to her teacher, she responds, "I am just bad and I make everybody crazy. My mom even wants to run away." Her mother wonders if a new school might be all she needs.

There is never one answer. Once again, it is the combination of parental involvement at home and school. Personalities vary with each and every one of us, and that's okay. However, building your child's self-perception, esteem, and drive to do his best starts with you.

"I want to be an architect and design the tallest building in the world." "Someday, I will be a Gator at the University of Florida studying business." "When I grow up I will be a famous chef and open my own restaurant." Do you know your child's dreams? Have you asked her about her hopes and desires? Parents must help children to dream big and feel that they are capable of being anything they want to be. We all know, as parents, that we support our children—just look at your bank account if, by any chance, you've forgotten. The critical part of parenting is to be sure that you are supporting them emotionally as well.

Often, without intention, we tear down our children's confidence and stamina to achieve. If children had to choose the most significant behaviors that their parents exhibited that made them feel the worst about themselves, they would name: being compared to siblings, threatening nonverbal gestures, showing hopelessness, and having no faith in them. These include expressions such as, "'Why can't you be more like your sister?' Mom shouted with the I am going choke you look." "I give up; I don't know what to do anymore." "Everyday I go to work to give you everything and all I ask is for you to try your best at school. Is that too much to ask?" "You didn't do your chores."

Our children perceive themselves greatly as we see them. You absolutely must show disappointment with them and correct them sometimes; however, you can discipline them without breaking their spirit, and you must make time to encourage and praise them for their accomplishments and efforts. Acknowledging you know they can and will do better often creates the desire to do so.

When your child looks in the mirror what does he see? When replaying discussions she had with you, is it encouraging or discouraging? Children, of course, need structure and discipline, but simultaneously they need to feel empowered and inspired. I am sure you are wondering how you can do that. I am going to tell you several of the ways you can build your children up, discipline them, and keep moving them in the right direction for success.

SECRET FOR SUCCESS #2: BELIEVE IN YOUR CHILDREN AND HELP THEM BELIEVE IN THEMSELVES!

Helping your child build a positive self-image is the key to successful parenting. Children begin to see themselves through the interactions they have with their parents. A child's self-esteem or self-worth will affect everything about him or her. What kind of friends they choose, how they get along with others, school performance, and how persistently they pursue their goals are all directly related to self-esteem. Children who have higher self-esteem have better attitudes about school, friends, parents, and their future.

Sometimes the job of parenting is frustrating, and it is tempting to resort to hurtful words and actions. What we say to our children is taken internally and affects how they feel about themselves. Statements such as: "What's wrong with you?" "I am ashamed of you!" and "You make me crazy" send the message that the child is a disappointment and foster a negative self-image. A parent's words stay with a child long after the parent has forgotten them. On the same note, positive statements build up children and engender positive views.

All children will drive you crazy at times and will definitely need discipline. When you need to reprimand and stop inappropriate behavior, it is essential you keep in mind that you can correct the problem without negative words. Building your child's self-esteem while teaching him what is right and wrong is difficult but possible. Let them know what they are doing is not appropriate and give consistent consequences without the negative expressions. Point out the positive behavior and discuss what would have been a better alternative. Apply punishment appropriately and follow through on realistic punishments. Encourage your child to be her best. Expressions such as, "You will do better next time," "I am disappointed but tomorrow is another day," and "I know you know better than that" show understanding and love. Don't forget the hugs and kisses that reassure children that although you may not be happy about an issue, you love them and together you can work out all issues and problems.

Self-esteem and self-respect go hand in hand. When it comes to parent–child relationships, "sticks and stones may break my bones but names can never hurt me" is absolutely incorrect. Children learn to love and respect themselves by having others love and respect them. Even when under stress and extreme frustration you should never put down your child. Help them feel good about themselves by listening to their concerns and discussing them. Share and express worries you had as a child. By sharing yourself, you will help them relate to you, and in turn, allow yourself to be an integral part of their lives when they need you most.

Encourage your children to feel comfortable with themselves, respect the differences in people, and practice healthy eating and living. Have them wear clothes that are comfortable, stylish, and make them feel good about themselves. Share with them experiences of feeling good, such as achieving in school, helping others, excelling at a hobby, or learning new things. Parents play an important role in helping children perceive themselves as unique and important individuals; remind them daily that you love them and believe in them and they will love and believe in themselves; that is the best antidote for low self-esteem. The lens your child looks through to see himself should reflect a positive view of his capabilities and future. Help them gain that sense of accomplishment. If they love to draw and excel in the arts, check your local newspaper and find out about contests and exhibitions they could enter. Everyone has special gifts and abilities; help your children find theirs.

Encourage your child to try different extracurricular activities until she finds something she will enjoy and at which she can excel. Sports teams, being a member of a club or organization help children feel important and included. Just remember to limit activities, as many children today are overscheduled. Think about the last time your child just played around the house doing nothing in particular. Research stresses the value of down time and not overscheduling children with extracurricular activities. Parents can achieve a balance between downtime, homework, studying, and extracurricular activities.

Before your child takes on any activities, sit down and make decisions regarding how many activities he should commit to and which hold a higher priority. Remind him they are all optional. As children grow, they will remember time spent with family rather than all the outside activities. The benefits of cuddling under a blanket, sharing a story, and just doing little things together mean more than you think.

Sometimes too many activities make children feel stressed as they race around worried about excelling at everything. Some children stay in an activity because they feel their parents expect it. When parents and their children discuss the activities and the time and commitment that accompany them, appropriate limits are reached.

Children need to be taught the meaning of respect for others. Respect and discipline go hand in hand. Parents will always have to discipline their children, but how you do it will determine your child's respect for you as well as for others. When a child does not listen or respond to a request, we can model mutual respect by delaying a privilege or pleasurable activity. Speak to your child in tones you would like to hear from him or her and listen when he speaks to you. Avoid criticizing to help teach your child about earning respect.

Minimize mistakes and focus on what they do right. Mistakes are just that, and hopefully we all learn from them. Express appreciation for positive behavior. Acknowledge progress and avoid demanding perfection. Your goal is to develop a well-rounded, educated lady or gentleman. Most of all, listen to your children's dreams and aspirations, excite them about their lives and futures, make them want to be all that they can be, and ensure them you will always be there for them.

Don't overreact to things they share with you or they will stop sharing. Make the effort to listen carefully, show interest, absorb the information, and take time to discuss it. Interrupting and interjecting comments will make them apprehensive to talk. Always encourage them to share what happened, before asking why. Always praise your children for sharing knowledge with you, even if unpleasant. Make them aware that you understand it was hard for them to tell you but that they made the right decision and, together, all obstacles can be overcome. This praise makes them excited about the next "bit of news" they can tell you. Avoid the use of negative or demeaning words. You may show disappointment with a certain behavior, but always let them know you love them and appreciate their honesty.

Children thrive on positive attention. Children need love and appreciation. Most parents find that it is easier to provide negative feedback rather than positive feedback. Find nice and approving things to say to your children so that when times arise to discipline or disagree, negativity will not be the majority of your conversations and you can work together toward solutions. Think back to your own childhood experiences, where the good times are often remembered but the bad times are unfortunately never forgotten.

GAINING THE PRIVATE SCHOOL EDGE: PRACTICAL TIPS, EXAMPLES, AND GUIDES TO GET YOU STARTED

Tip #1: Praise your child. Believe in him or her. Give positive attention. Help him or her find something to excel in and feel good about.

Sean, Age 11

Sean's little brother, Mike, is smart as a whip; everyone says so. He also excels at sports and just about anything he attempts. Mike is funny and outgoing and every time adults meet him they tell his parents, "You have the next president on your hands. You're going to have the girls breaking down the door for this little guy." As parents, they can't keep the large smiles and overwhelming pride they have in Mike off their faces. They love their sons and worry about Sean and wonder why he seems uninterested in any sports or hobbies and is quite reserved

Advice for Getting Sean on the Right Track

Sean's parents should expose him to different activities to help him develop interests and find "his thing." He needs something he can enjoy, excel at, and learn. Sean needs to experience a sense of belonging, a feeling of accomplishment, and the joy of success.

Your Current Situation: Where Are You Now?

Ask yourself these questions and reflect on the answers:

- Do you know your child's interests?
- Do you compare your child to siblings or other children?

- Do you know your child's favorite hobby?
- When was the last time you complimented your child?
- Do you encourage your child to participate in any sports or clubs?

Tip #2: Minimize mistakes. Expect their best not the best. Award effort.

Samantha, Age 12

Samantha really wants to please her parents. She always pays attention in class and thinks she understands the material the teacher is going over. Every time she takes a test she comes home feeling good about the results. When she gets the test back, there are many errors, and the grade is poor to say the least. When she takes it home, her parents are less than pleased. Samantha feels "stupid" and has started to hate school. Her parents remind her constantly that doing

Create a list of your child's positive characteristics.
_____
_____
_____
_____

Create a list of your child's hobbies/interests.
_____
_____
_____
_____

Create a list of activities your child would like to try.
_____
_____
_____
_____

Setting the Expectation: You will try your best with persistence, determination, and drive.

Reaching the Goal: You raised your grade; way to go.

Making It a Priority: Schoolwork is a priority, and you can do it. Struggling sometimes occurs, but we will get there. You can do it.

well in school is all that is asked of her, and they always look disappointed.

Advice for Getting Samantha on the Right Track

When a test comes home from school, Samantha's parents should review it with her and go over the questions she missed. Reflecting on mistakes is often a great way to learn. The source of the errors should be discovered to prevent making them in the future. Her parents should offer praise for her effort. Statements such as "Now we discovered where the mistakes were, and you will certainly do better next time" will help Samantha feel confident on the next exam. Maybe she really knows the material, and you as the parent must find out where her weaknesses lie.

CHAPTER 3

Educating Children about At-Risk Behaviors

Not my son, he would never do drugs. We talk about drugs and he knows they're bad.

REAL STORIES AND FEARS

Melissa, Age 10

Melissa has been offered cigarettes, both legal and illegal. She never told her mother. Once when she went to her friend Monica's house, Bianca, the older sister, was smoking pot and told both the girls to try it and then laughed and locked them out of her room. Melissa's mom has heard about how important it is to talk to your children about drugs, but knew her daughter was of course much too young for such talk. Have you ever thought about at what age you should be discussing substance abuse and that maybe what you thought of as "too young" really isn't. Don't assume anything; have firsthand knowledge.

Kristen, Age 11

Kristen is on a softball team. She overhears other girls, who go to public school, talking about how they do drugs in the bathroom during school. She asks them if they ever got in trouble and they tell her nobody pays attention. They even said boys go into the bathroom, too. All you have to do is tell the teacher you have to go to the bathroom and then all meet up. Sometimes, as parents, we think "not my child." Remember, don't close your eyes; check and recheck every aspect of your child's life. Remind your child it's not what you get away with; it's what you should and should not get involved with.

Marlene, Age 13

Marlene cuts school and goes home with a couple of friends. They watch movies, and when asked if she worries about getting caught, she says, "My dad doesn't care; he watches with us." Marlene goes wild at parties, gets drunk; her mom picks her up, but she never gets punished. Her friends describe her mother as "clueless." They say Marlene is allowed to do whatever she wants because no one seems to notice her behavior. She gets Cs and Ds in school and her parents joke about how at least she is not failing. Who is in her corner to set the proper example? No one? Are you in your children's corner in helping them reach their potential? Do you say, "do as I do," or just "do as I say." Remember, only you can set the proper example.

Tatiana, Age 14

Tatiana goes to a private school. When she goes to parties, only sodas are served. There are always chaperones at all functions. You get reprimanded for dancing too close; no one would dare drink or do drugs. Before they attend, kids know what is expected of them and what the consequences are for inappropriate behavior. Parents know their children's friends and their friend's parents. Better to be a little overprotective than underprotective or not protective at all.

Stephanie, Age 10

Stephanie is in the movie theater watching a film about a girl who took drugs, got involved with an older man, and ended up getting arrested. She whispered to her neighbor, "That same thing happened to my friend. She even got kicked out of school." How familiar are you with your child's friends? Share their lives and their stories. The company your child keeps has a great influence on his behavior and his actions.

For Your Information

- 73% of ninth grade students had at least one drink of alcohol on one or more days during their lifetimes. (National Center for Chronic Disease Prevention and Health Promotion, 2001)
- 29% of students had their first drink of alcohol other than a few sips before age 13. (National Center for Chronic Disease Prevention and Health Promotion, 2001)
- 30% of high school students had five or more drinks of alcohol in a row, that is, within a couple of hours, on one or more of the past 30 days. (National Center for Chronic Disease Prevention and Health Promotion, 2001)
- 24% of high school students used marijuana one or more times during the past 30 days. (National Center for Chronic Disease Prevention and Health Promotion, 2001)
- 29% of 9th graders were offered, sold, or given an illegal drug on school property by someone during the past 12 months. (National Center for Chronic Disease Prevention and Health Promotion, 2001)
- 53% of adolescents have tried an illicit drug by the time they finish high school. (Johnston et al., 2004)
- Nearly 4 out of 5 of teenagers have consumed alcohol and 47% have done so by 8th grade. (Johnston et al., 2004)
- Nearly half of all 8th graders and three-quarters of all 10th graders reported marijuana as being accessible. (Johnston et al., 2004)
- 95% of 12th graders reported alcohol as being accessible. (Johnston et al., 2004)

SECRET FOR SUCCESS #3: TALK ABOUT AT-RISK BEHAVIORS NOW AND GET TO KNOW THEIR FRIENDS

Drugs and Alcohol

Unfortunately, experimentation with alcohol and drugs during childhood is common. Even scarier is that children often don't see the link between their actions today and the consequences tomorrow. They often feel indestructible and adopt the attitude that bad things don't happen to them. Research suggests that using alcohol and tobacco at a young age increases the risk of using other drugs later. Teens use alcohol and other drugs for many reasons, including but not limited to curiosity, feeling good, stress, peer pressure, or to defy authority. Young adults who come from families with a history of drug or alcohol abuse experience depression and develop low self-esteem and are usually at a greater risk for the same problems.

Parental involvement seems to be a significant factor in helping children say no to drugs. Parents must be the "watchdogs" of their children and be well informed in prevention, detection, and education regarding drugs. There is nothing like the fear of disappointing parents and severe consequences to keep you focused on what is right and knowledgeable of what is clearly unacceptable. The influence of parents is the most underutilized tool in preventing youth substance abuse.

Today, there is a variety of drugs, both legal and illegal. Among the legally available drugs are alcohol, prescribed medications, inhalants (fumes from glues, aerosols, and solvents) and over-the-counter cough, cold, sleep, and diet medications. The most commonly used illegal drugs are marijuana (pot), stimulants (cocaine, crack, and speed), LSD, PCP, opioids, heroin, and designer drugs, like Ecstasy. Research suggests that the average age of first marijuana and alcohol use can be before age 12. Drug use is associated with school failure, distorted judgment, accidents, mood swings, incidences of violence, and unplanned and unsafe sex.

Parents can and should provide early communication and education to their children. Parents must also be aware and look for signs of teenage alcohol and drug abuse. Never assume; really know. Common indicators are: fatigue, poor health, mood swings, depression, withdrawal from the family, a general lack of interest, and isolation behavior. When your child has been out with friends, be sure to greet him when he gets home. Look in his eyes to see if they are glossy, red, or dull. Sometimes you may be able to smell tobacco or other products on her clothing or in her hair. Drugs and alcohol usually arouse defiant and argumentative behavior, leading to a poor self-image, unhappiness, and discontentment. If your child seems to undergo a personality change, you may want to investigate her recent activities, acquaintances, and the reasons for this change. Don't assume its just the teen years and it will pass.

School is affected by the use of drugs and alcohol. A negative attitude and a lack of interest will usually occur. Absences, cases of truancy, declining grades, discipline problems, and the appearance of new friends are signs of trouble. Problems with the law may also occur. The sooner you catch substance abuse and nip it in the bud, the better the odds are of it not reoccurring.

Sometimes kids feel that alcohol is a legal and safe alternative to "real drugs." It is important to remind them that alcohol is a powerful, mood-altering drug that impairs judgment and that the risks associated with alcohol abuse are many. Teens who drink have an increased risk of death by car accidents, drowning, suicide, and homicide. They are more likely to become sexually active at earlier ages and experience increased incidences of unprotected sex. An individual who begins drinking as a young teen is four times more likely to develop alcohol dependence than those who don't drink. During the past decade, higher levels of early sexual activity, unplanned pregnancies, and sexually transmitted diseases have been reported. To reduce the incidence of these problems in the future, discussions of alcohol and other drug abuse must be a parent's priority and a parent's duty. Unfortunately, it is highly likely that your child will be offered alcohol and/or drugs at some point. You can make him prepared to say no. Make your expectations clear and support your child. Common sense and communication are the best ways to assist your child in handling these types of situations. Be certain your child knows she can call you at anytime to pick her up without being scolded or embarrassed. Give them examples of ways to say no and let them feel comfortable blaming you. Remind your child that your shoulders are big and strong and he can always use the quote, "My mother would kill me if I did that."

Friends and At-Risk Behaviors

The job of parenting goes beyond just observing your own children. Knowing their friends is key. Through their friends, you may find out what interests and influences your children. Typically, a close friend shares important interests your child cares about and is exposed to. As parents, we must communicate about friendships and the characteristics of a good friend. The earlier we start these talks the more likely they will continue into the teen years, when children need the support, guidance, and help of loving parents.

Your home should be a place where your child's friends feel welcome and your child feels comfortable inviting them. This allows you to spend more time observing your child and her friends. With each grade level, peer pressure becomes a larger part of your child's academic and social life. Around third grade, having a best friend becomes important. This brings great joy but has the potential for hurt. It is normal for children to experience ups and downs, but it is usually not necessary to get heavily involved.

Assure your child you are happy he has friends and explain what your expectations of friendships are. Good parenting begins with being a good listener. However, if you feel one of your child's friends is having a negative influence, you should make your child aware of it. Discuss the situation and put it in its right perspective while being totally understanding. Steering your child from friends engaging in destructive behaviors is your job and your right. Remind her friendship should be about helping one another succeed and making positive choices. Remember, you may get to know your child better by spending time getting to know her peers; all this leads to sharing and understanding.

Children often depend more on peers for emotional support and advice than do adults, so their friends can be influential when it comes to at-risk behaviors. Peer pressure is the pressure we feel to be like other people. It sometimes is a positive thing that plays a big role in determining who we are. However, peer pressure can be a negative force in the lives of children and adolescents that results in unpleasant and life-threatening consequences. Peer pressure is more than a phase that results in hard to accept hairstyles, body piercing, or clothing. Peer pressure is a powerful reality and must be addressed by parents to teach their children responsible decision making.

Research supports the conclusion that parents do have a powerful influence over their children and adolescents. Parents must help them defend themselves from the negative effects of peer pressure. All people young and old make numerous decisions every day both simple and difficult. Young people must be taught responsible decision making, including how to refuse negative offers. Making children comfortable with what they say and do is essential. Role-playing peer-pressure situations with children is a helpful and effective way to help them. Talk about how to avoid undesirable situations or people who break the rules or participate in undesirable behavior.

Peer pressure is not usually blatant. Peers won't just walk up to each other and say, "Here, smoke this." It is usually a desire by a child to do something, to feel included or accepted by his peers. Unfortunately, peers typically outrank the family as the center of a young person's life. Parents must strive to remain an active and integral part of their children's lives. Communication and prioritizing time spent together can lessen the distancing that occurs as children grow and strengthen the family bonds.

Self-confidence can help children stand firm, walk away, and resist doing something harmful to themselves. Talking about appropriate choices and role-playing real-life scenarios may be the best defense against peer pressure. Encourage your child to join a friend who you know is above peer pressure and sets a good example for your child and shares the same goals and achievement. There is strength in numbers. Remind them, if they stand their ground and do what they know is right, they will make the best choices for themselves and a have a world of opportunities ahead of them. One mistake can lead to lifetime of regret and repercussions.

GAINING THE PRIVATE SCHOOL EDGE: PRACTICAL TIPS, EXAMPLES, AND GUIDES TO GET YOU STARTED

Tip #1: Set a good example. Talk about right from wrong. Start talking about drugs and alcohol early. Don't be afraid to discuss with them the consequences of bad and dangerous behavior. Role-play refusing negative offers. Be a good listener. Don't overreact . . . just react.

Gabby, Age 13

Gabby snuck out of her house and was riding around in her boyfriend's car. He was pulled over for speeding, and they were both arrested for possession of marijuana. Gabby's boyfriend tested positive for being under the influence. Gabby's parents were horrified.

Advice for Getting Gabby on the Right Track

Gabby's parents should educate themselves on drug use in children and teens. They should have her tested at their doctor and get her some counseling.

Your Current Situation: Where Are You Now?

Ask yourself these questions and reflect on the answers:

- Has your child ever been exposed to drugs?
- Do any of your children's friends drink or do drugs?
- Does your son or daughter have a boyfriend of girlfriend?
- Does your child ride in someone else's car without your permission?
- When is the last time you had a conversation about drugs and alcohol with your children?

Joe, Age 14

Joe really wants to be cool. He wants to have a lot of friends and make kids laugh. One day after school, Joe invites a couple of friends over. They start drinking beer, and Joe gives them a couple of tequila shots from the bar in the dining room. Joe's mom comes home and finds one of the glasses broken in the garbage can. After questioning her husband, she realizes something is going on with Joe.

Advice for Getting Joe on the Right Track

Joe's parents need to sit down and have a serious conversation. Having friends over and serving alcohol without permission is totally unacceptable. Besides the fact that serving alcohol to minors is against the law, Joe's vision of "cool" must be restructured within acceptable limits.

Create a list of the qualities of a good friend.

_____
_____
_____
_____

Create a list of your child's friends.

_____
_____
_____
_____

CHAPTER 4

Parental Involvement

You determine and define the meaning of success for your child. If success in school is required and doing your best is the mission, all children will reach their potential. You, as the parent, must be the cheerleader when things get tough, never stopping until you've reached the finish line. We cannot make excuses when our children don't succeed but rather must lay the groundwork for the path to brighter days. Parents who never demonstrate quitting raise children who don't quit. Parent's who try their best raise children who try their best. We have all heard the saying, Behind every successful man is a good woman. Well, I can tell you that behind every successful student is a concerned and involved parent. You can be the factor that determines whether your child strives for excellence or settles for getting by and takes the path of least resistance.

REAL STORIES AND FEARS

Barbara, Mother of Three

She has a house in a nice neighborhood and three children she believes to be on their way to successful futures. Little does she know her daughter, age 13, roams the neighborhood, hanging out with older teenagers while she is sound asleep. Mom works all day, comes home to cook and clean, and is in bed by nine at night. Her daughter knows how to prop the garage door to get in and out undetected. It was no surprise to her friends when she had to drop out of school because of an unwanted pregnancy. Are you sure you know where your children are? Are you spontaneous with supervision? Have your children earned your full trust, and when should you put your guard down?

Angela, Age 12

Her schoolwork used to be the center of discussion at the dinner table, but now she feels schoolwork isn't that important to her or anyone else. She feels sad that her mom has to work so much that it makes her tired and inaccessible. No one seems to bring up school or inquire about school progress or grades. Do you ask your children about school issues ranging from friends and grades to their hopes and dreams?

Monica, Mother of Two

Monica works hard to keep her children clothed and fed and to give them most of what they want. She doesn't understand why they can't repay her and just do well in school. Their teachers say they are unmotivated and don't try their best. She constantly feels like she sacrifices so much for them. She relies on the notion that they should automatically be good and do well in school to repay her. Monica needs a different approach and needs to get involved in her children's schooling. It's wrong to assume children will just do the right thing. Doing the right thing is learned from parental love and guidance.

SECRET FOR SUCCESS #4: BE INVOLVED

Parents must strive to create a home environment that encourages the wonder and joy of learning and stay active. Being involved in your child's education doesn't mean you have to miss work and volunteer in the school. Parent–child conversations about school events show children that you are interested and concerned in what they learn. Activities that inspire learning, such as educational trips and reading to, and with, them make a huge difference. Student achievement improves when parents express realistic expectations, shared goals, and plans to achieve them.

When parents come to school regularly, it reinforces the idea that home and school are connected, and that school and its importance are integral parts of the whole family's life. Try to attend as many parent–school activities, such as parents association meetings, extracurricular activities, athletics, school plays, and assemblies, as often as possible. Take an active role in your child's homework and test preparation. Make sure that homework assigned to your child is completed. Limit time spent watching TV during the week so additional time may be spent on studying and reading. Model the value of learning, self-discipline, and hard work. Encourage and trace your child's development and progress in school.

Maintaining a warm and supportive home that shows interest in children's progress at school and encourages them is vital. Helping with homework, discussing the value of a good education and possible career options, and staying in touch with teachers make all the difference in a child's achievement. Children achieve higher grades when parents monitor their daily activities, keep close track on their progress in school, and maintain open communication. A more focused parental involvement, aimed at encouraging students to spend more time on homework, might well lead indirectly to higher grades. Reading, listening to your child read, and discussing what is being read aid in learning.

The research is overwhelmingly clear: When parents play a positive role in their children's education, children do better in school. This is true whether or not parents are college educated and regardless of the family income, race, or ethnic background. What counts is that parents have a positive attitude about the importance of a good education and that they express confidence that their children can and will succeed. Some major benefits of parent involvement include higher grades and test scores, positive attitudes and better behavior.

The teacher part of me suggests that all parents should do this homework assignment: Write down your view of your child's school habits. Be sure to include homework and studying skills, responsibility, organization, and effort level. Then write down improvements you would like to see.

Parents are a major influence in helping their children become responsible and capable human beings. They must believe they can and should help their children fulfill the high aspirations they have for them by helping with homework, meeting with their teachers, and expecting their best. The most important role for parents is to value and teach the value of educational experiences. Parents do not have to be well educated themselves to help. Research supports that almost any form of parental involvement appears to improve student performance. Stay in frequent contact with the school and communicate to children daily that you believe in them and you expect nothing but their best.

Parents should set the standard for fulfilling commitments and obligations. When children are taught that quitting or giving up is an option, they are given a choice to succeed or not to succeed. Do as I say not as I do does not work with children. "I started going to the gym but am too busy to carry it out" sets the stage for unfinished business. Show your child you are dedicated to follow through on everything you do. It is okay to let them see you struggle, but work harder and remain true to the task until the task is completed.

If your child has an interest in a sport, instrument, or some other hobby, by all means enroll her. If she starts to get bored or frustrated, make her stick it out to the end of the season, year, or equivalent. Children must learn that once you make a commitment, you must fulfill your end of the bargain. School must be looked at as a commitment, and success is the only option. We, as parents, must be actively involved in the process of keeping our children on the right path. The parents steer the child in the right direction and keep him steady on shaky ground. You would certainly not let your child dart across a busy road, so you shouldn't allow them behaviors that inhibit school success.

GAINING THE PRIVATE SCHOOL EDGE: PRACTICAL TIPS, EXAMPLES, AND GUIDES TO GET YOU STARTED

Tip #1: Look over their homework and monitor their studying. Keep close track of their school progress and grades. Show interest in your child's school day. Attend school activities. Read to, and with, your children and discuss what you have read.

Colton, Age 9

Colton comes home each day from school and says he has no homework or that he did it in school. His mother just smiles and says okay. Colton does rush through his homework while at school to avoid having to carry home his books or waste precious "play time." He spends little time studying and preparing for exams. At report card time, his grades are passing but far from honor roll or even satisfactory.

Advice for Getting Colton on the Right Track

Colton's parents need to contact his teacher and become informed. They should be familiar with the homework policy and the test schedule. Colton needs reminding when he has an exam. His parents should review the material with him and ask him questions. His homework should be looked at daily, even when he completes it in school.

Your Current Situation: Where Are You Now?

Ask yourself these questions and reflect on the answers:

- Do I discuss my child's school day?
- When was the last time I went to a school event?
- How much time should my child spend on homework?
- Do I encourage my child to try his best?
- How well does my child get along with others?
- Is my child working up to his or her ability?
- Does my child participate in class discussions and ask questions?
- Is my child a good test taker?
- Do I read to my child regularly?

Tip #2: Visit museums and plan educational trips to show a passion for learning. Order newspapers and magazines. Share positive attitudes about teachers and subjects. Discuss the value of a good education and career options. Help make learning fun and interesting.

Justina, Age 7

Justina never seems interested in anything. When asked what she learned in school, she responds "Stuff." She rarely asks questions or talks about things she would like to see or do.

Advice for Getting Justina on the Right Track

Justina needs her curiosity triggered. Her parents should allow for experiences that allow her to get excited about learning. Bake a cake and teach measurement. Make Jell-O and talk about solids and liquids. Let Justina count out the money when shopping and make the change. Take Justina to the library and let her research a topic of her choice.

Many parents have demanding careers and heavy social calendars. We sometimes tell ourselves that we need to time to socialize with other adults, do charity work, and have some of our own interests. Yes, it's true, parents are people too and need some time. However, our children need and crave family time together. Put your children first, as they are young for such a short time. No one, and nothing, can replace you, your love, and your interest in them.

Describe your current practice of parent involvement.

_____

_____

_____

_____

Reaching the Goal: Compile of list of questions to ask your child each day when she gets home from school.

Example: What was the most interesting thing you learned in school today?

_____

_____

_____

_____

Making It a Priority: Parental involvement pledge—Obtain a school calendar and record school meetings and events. Make a list of those you will attend this year.

_____

_____

_____

CHAPTER 5

Effective Organization

In my childhood home, organization was a way of life. Everything had its place in the house, from the brooms, to the pots and pans, to our shoes and socks. We knew where everything went, and every time we used something, we were required to put it back in its exact spot, and in fact, in its exact condition. Sharing a room with my sister was not always an easy task. Often, things would start to look a mess, and when they did, my mom had the solution. She used to dump out all of our drawers, leave them in the center of the room and we couldn't leave until everything in the room was in its exact place. There were no junk drawers or areas for things for which you didn't have a place. If things didn't belong somewhere, we didn't need them and we got rid of them. I remember feeling tortured in that prison of organization growing up, but right now, even though I don't tell my mom, I thank her every day for raising me to be organized. I think it is one of the biggest secrets to my own personal success.

REAL STORIES AND FEARS

Brandon, Age 7

When it comes time to do homework each day, Brandon's mom feels like she is going to have a nervous breakdown. He never remembers all his books, and he writes down the wrong page numbers for his assignments, when he even bothers to write them down at all. She feels helpless and blames herself for his behavior. Punishing him doesn't seem to help him get it together. Some people do not know they are disorganized until they are organized.

SECRET FOR SUCCESS #5: DEVELOP GOOD ORGANIZATIONAL SKILLS

Disorganization can and usually does affect a child's performance in every aspect. Parents who help a child to become organized ease the road to higher education.

Model Appropriate Behavior

Organization is something that is achieved over time. If children see organized parents, they will begin to learn by example. Let them see you arranging the kitchen cabinets, making grocery lists, and straightening out the closets. Start early with their toys; let them help you put them away where they belong. This is how organization is learned.

We all know that life is often a juggling act, balancing kids, family, career, and whatever else comes our way. Organization is really what determines if we succeed and how we feel by the end of the day. In our closets, it's the shoes being lined up and easy to locate; it's laying out our clothes the night before school, thinking about what we are going to have for meals, and planning what we need for the day. All these things go a long way to helping maintain our mental and physical health. Organization and planning all make for an easy flow on a day-to-day basis. Our children follow in our footsteps and mimic this behavior.

As parents, we must model behavior that is going to lead our children to be consistent and organized. This is one of the biggest things that we can do for them in regard to school. I don't ever remember a time when I came home from school and looked for a snack and it wasn't there. Being organized, even with simple things like groceries, let my mom know, oh, we're out of this or we're out of that, and everything was replaced in a timely fashion. We also never had the problem of having outdated canned goods because everything was clearly visible and everything was rotated. This may sound trivial, but organizing is a family affair, and the importance of organization must show through every single thing we do, from how we place our clothes and shoes to how we organize our kitchen cabinets. To-do lists and shopping lists echo organization. This, in turn, is taught to our children so homework assignments and projects are recorded, planned, and tracked. Notes and important things that teachers tell students are recorded and thus remembered.

It's never too early to start your child with organization, because from the time they are two years old, children can learn where things go by taking part in simple activities like cleaning up and this toy goes in this bucket and that toy goes in that bucket. Having buckets labeled, with different sizes and colors, lets children know where things belong. Making to-do lists is something simple that we can formulate into a habit, ensuring our kids never forget something important, and doing it allows them great satisfaction when they complete tasks. There is nothing like making that long list of things to do and then being able to scratch out items and go, "Wow, I'm done."

Dry erase boards don't have to be just for school. There is something fun about writing on that little board—lists, menus, and all different things that can help children to learn organization and planning. What are we going to have for dinner tonight? Have your child help make a balanced meal. Write down what materials are needed, what you have and what you have to buy. All of these sorts of everyday things that we do can lead a child to organization.

When you're making your shopping list, your children can be involved. When they are old enough, you can send them into their bathroom and say, Make a list of what you need. Do you have shampoo, toothpaste, and any other bathroom products that are necessary?

Organization can also be taught through trash. Recycle bins help children sort and put items in their proper places. Get your children involved to determine what goes where, what can be saved, and what gets thrown away. Without any particular skill in education or teaching, you, as someone who runs a household, can teach your children to be organized and the joy that comes with it.

Many of us today live by tight schedules, especially in regard to our children. With school, soccer practice and ballet, and the fact that often our children are going to different places at the same time, we all know the value in organization. We want our children to use an agenda or planner at school so we need to model it at home. Placing a big family calendar and writing everybody's activities down shows your children, through example, that writing down items and keeping a calendar is the way that you get things done. If you work, you manage your career, home, and that important job of parenting, as well as all your other responsibilities. Children learn by example, and organization is one of those traits they learn through watching you and experiencing with you. When they see their parents consistently running around looking for keys, looking for materials, having to go back to find something they've forgotten, they often learn the same. When they see parents who pack bags prior to an event, make a list of items needed, and pre-plan who is going to pick up and drop off, they learn planning and organization.

If you're like me and have to be five places at the same time, organization is the only way to manage day to day. We, as parents, can give children the great gift of organization and make our lives easier by modeling and living the life of organization.

As a classroom teacher and an administrator, I have heard the excuses for not being prepared for school, not having a book, not having homework—"I did it, but I left it at home." "I put it in the wrong folder." "I had it, and I don't remember what I did with it." "I promise you. I even remember some of the answers." You can help your child avoid these types of events in school by getting him to be organized with his folders and by always having a place for each subject and by putting things in their proper places. Don't save it for later. When you complete your homework, put it in your homework folder. Gather the homework folder and put it in your backpack; not I'll do it later, because we all are very busy and we may forget. Too many times I have heard, "I left it on the printer in my computer. I was working on it on my desk. I was going to check it over one more time and I left it behind." Not only does that frustrate you as the parent who knows your child did her homework and didn't get credit for it or received late credit, but it also frustrates the child. He did his work and gave it his best; and he didn't even get to turn it in. Or sometimes it's in their backpacks and they don't remember where they put it. That's when all that color coding and folders and labeling come to life.

Teach your children about labeling trays, folders, all types of things by doing it in your home. Most people have a clothes basket or bins for toys. Everything has its place at home, just as it should at school. Homework goes in one folder. Math goes in another folder. Every subject has its spot; not everything shoved in the backpack. Again, I say to you as a teacher and administrator I see this all the time, and it hinders children. This is something we can fix. Sometimes a child might struggle with a subject area or a certain part of some subject and you may not be able to help them with that. You might need outside assistance, such as a tutor. Organization, however, is something at which we can be successful, and we should help our children with their organization because it is something that needs to be embedded and learned and followed through every single day of a child's life.

By getting our children organized we can also help them find time for some fun and relaxation. Today, children run from school to activities, whether it's clubs, sports, or aftercare facilities, until we come home from work, and they don't have time to just unwind from a busy day of listening and learning. When we put a schedule on paper and we organize our time, children have more time to be children, and this is essential. Sometimes children go, go, go and are overscheduled and can't perform at their best because they don't have time to clear their minds and just do nothing. Time management can help a child achieve by allowing time for adequate rest, relaxation, meals, and, of course, pleasure reading and learning.

Research confirms the value of downtime and of not overscheduling children. Parents can achieve a balance between downtime, homework, study, and extracurricular activities. Children need some unstructured free time in which to think, create, and experience being a kid. Reading under a tree and just daydreaming have healthy benefits. Families have little time together due to necessities of life. Shared meals and relaxing are dwindling as parents rush to sports activities and ballet lessons. In the past two decades, national studies have indicated that structured sports time has doubled, unstructured activities declined by 50%, household conversations are far less frequent, family dinners declined 33%, and family vacations decreased by 28%.

Learning needs to be made fun. Learning needs to be seen as an avenue to relax and get excited all at the same time. So after the school day is done and the homework is done and the extracurricular activities are done, we hope to have some time for relaxed learning, like reading a novel or watching an informative program. Kids need time for learning just to learn and not for grades or tests.

If you look around your home right now and find that you have a lot of organizing to do before you can get your child on track, that's okay. Start today. We can start with that drawer in the kitchen that many of us know far too well, the drawer where we stuff everything because we might need it. Papers from school, bits of papers with phone numbers, pieces of mail. That drawer that is accessible to anyone. One day, pull it out and get organized. For example, place mail to review here and things to file there. Phone numbers go here. Important messages go here. Little by little, as we organize our children and we become more organized, life just gets easier and more manageable. As parents, we know there are often times that we feel, "How am I going to get through another day to accomplish everything I need to accomplish?" Put it down on paper and just get started one thing at a time. Cross out as you go along to help you keep your sanity and know that all is manageable. This helps you, but more important, teaches your children that they can manage everything as well. Even when things seem to be piling up and there are tests and there are projects and all types of things that they need to get done, if we organize and tackle one thing at a time, it can be done. Little by little, with a list, get started and you've mastered half the battle. "Okay, I'm going to do this at this time, this at that time," and it all seems conquerable.

Prioritizing goes right along with organizing. Children, like adults, will find there are many things they have to do. Let them take a look at due dates, the amount of time something is going to take, and organize: this should be done first; this should be done second; this can wait until the weekend. Prioritizing helps children get things done efficiently and with minimal stress. This is something that we must teach them, something we must live and model.

Organizing is learning to make a plan. Whether you're a second grader in school or a CEO of a big corporation, making plans helps you get the job done, no matter how big or how small. From the big advertising plan for a company to the science fair project for your second grader, make a plan. "This weekend we're going to collect the materials." "On Wednesday afternoon before baseball practice we're going to go to the library and check out some books on the topic area." "On Saturday, we're going to have Uncle Bob over to help us build the board and carry on from there." When you break down big tasks for your little people, they become easier to manage and a lot more exciting. Then, the dreaded science fair project becomes a series of fun little events, giving ample time to complete it without pressure, without raised voices, and without taking a toll on the entire family.

School Supplies and Work Area

For school, provide your children with all the necessary supplies. Teach organization by showing them how to prepare materials and where to place them so they are easily accessible. Designate an area for your children to do homework and study. The space should be clutter free. Drawers and shelves should be filled neatly with supplies, current papers, and works in progress. Provide a file for the year's schoolwork. Help your child clean and organize his backpack, notebook, and desk. Require he put all books, notebooks, signed notes, and other necessary materials inside the backpack and place it in the same place each night.

Homework and Home Environment

Parents should try to provide structure and routine in the home environment. Teach children to get used to placing things in their proper places so they are easy to locate when needed. Laying out clothes and packing book bags teaches wise use of time and removes pressure from them. Set a consistent schedule for homework and establish a daily routine with expectations clearly defined and discussed in the family. Be sure that their friends know when homework and study time is and that they should not call during that time. On that same note, be sure your kids have a phone number of a responsible student to ask questions about homework when necessary. Remind children to check their assignments and obtain all necessary books and notebooks before they leave school.

Homework time must also allow for reading and studying. Help your child keep track of papers by organizing notebooks. Use dividers to separate notes, classwork, homework, etc. Completed papers should be kept in a file at home so children can easily locate current work in their notebooks.

Time Management

Getting things done in a timely fashion, meeting deadlines, and using calendars and schedules are important tools for school and life. Assist your child with prioritization of activities and workload. Breaking down assignments and projects into manageable increments is crucial to ensuring completion and success. Monitor their progress and do not allow procrastination, which leads to inadequate results and stress. A reasonable time should be dedicated to homework. Checklists are great tools for children. They should be used to list assignments, needed materials, schoolbooks, and household chores. Crossing items off the list will help them take ownership of their responsibilities and instill a sense of accomplishment for completing tasks. Keep a calendar for the household and check it regularly. Mark the family's activities and events, school dates, assignment due dates, and tests. Set the example by filling out important things you have to remember. An organization board in the kitchen is a great idea. Make it a fun project with your child. Provide sections for household chores, school, and a to-do list. Use different colors for different members of the family. Make organization a fun family affair.

Time to discuss a child's school day is becoming rare. This time cannot be recaptured. Before your child takes on any activities, sit down and make decisions regarding how many activities he should commit to and which hold a higher priority. Remind him that all are optional. As children grow, they will remember time spent with family rather than all the outside activities. The benefits of cuddling, sharing a story, and doing little things together are great and will resonate. Too many activities can make children feel stressed as they race around, worried about excelling at everything. Some children stay in an activity because they feel their parents expect it. When parents and children discuss activities and the time and commitment that accompany them, appropriate limits are reached. Remember, organization includes balancing life to allow time for your child to relax and for family members to enjoy one another.

Organization is a skill that must be taught and modeled with patience and guidance. Assisting children at a young age to form organizational skills can only help them and can also help you.

GAINING THE PRIVATE SCHOOL EDGE: PRACTICAL TIPS, EXAMPLES, AND GUIDES TO GET YOU STARTED

Tip #1: Model organization. Keep a regular household schedule. Require use of a daily planner.

Ricky, Age 12

Ricky started middle school and promised his mother it would be a great year. There were six subjects with six different teachers and he had to change classes. After four weeks of school, progress reports were sent home. Ricky was failing three out of six subjects, and it seemed to be from a failure to turn in homework. After heated arguments, it was determined that Ricky had done most of his homework but often did not turn it in because he was unable to locate it at collection time.

Advice for Getting Ricky on the Right Track

Ricky needs separate notebooks and folders for each subject area. These notebooks should be labeled and have sections for homework, classwork, and notes. Each night after he completes his homework, it should be filed in the right place. Ricky's parents need to check his backpack and school supplies periodically to be sure he is keeping his notebooks organized.

Your Current Situation: Where Are You Now?

Ask yourself these questions and reflect on the answers:

- Does your child have a folder/notebook for each subject?
- Does your child pack her backpack the night before?
- Does your child keep a list of assignments with due dates?

- Does your child check his backpack for all books and notebooks he must bring home each day?
- Do you check her school notebooks periodically?

Tip #2: Include children in cleaning and organization of the home. Avoid overscheduling your children. Allow time for relaxation.

Liz, Age 8

Liz's room looks like a tornado hit. Her closet has toys thrown everywhere. Her drawers are stuffed, and locating shoes and socks is often a challenge. It is no wonder that her papers coming from school look like they survived a war. When it comes time to prepare for a test in school, she usually can't find her notes or study guides from the teacher.

Advice for Getting Liz on the Right Track

Liz's parents need to begin the process of organization in her room. Organization is a skill that must be followed through in all aspects of a child's life. A person does not have an organized office and a disorganized home. They should help Liz organize her room and schoolbooks and follow up with frequent checkups.

Life, and especially school, calls for students to be responsible and organized. One of the biggest obstacles to school success is a lack of planning and organization that allows the children proper time management to complete all tasks and study. Parents can and should model and demand organization in every aspect of their children's lives. Start today!

Describe the current practice in your home. Rate your own organizational skills and make a list of things to start you on the road to organization.

_____

_____

_____

_____

Create an Organization "To Do" List

Your Expectations: The ideal situation.

Example: Organize all notebooks and create an organization board.

_____

_____

_____

_____

Reaching the Goal: Using your current organizational system as a baseline, set goals to get yourself organized and to set a schedule to allow time for everything.

Example: I will organize all my notebooks and make a schedule to include homework, studying, extracurricular activities, and adequate rest.

_____

_____

_____

_____

Making It a Priority: Be the model and keeper of organization.

Example: Everything has its place and all family members must keep it that way.

_____

_____

_____

_____

_____

CHAPTER 6

Values

REAL STORIES AND FEARS

Kara, Age 13

Her soccer team has players from all different schools. Every practice and every game she is shocked at the lack of sportsmanship and always thinks, "These kids should be thankful they don't go to my school or have my parents; they would kill me for talking like that." Many parents listen to their children curse profusely when they miss the ball and sympathize with them. Sometimes parents join in when they are cursing at the coach or referee. You set the example in raising ladies and gentlemen, and teaching self-control and proper behavior is paramount.

Cathy, Age 11

"Parents at my school are all the same. They come to every game and event we go to. My friends from my soccer team are so lucky. Their parents drop them off and let them do all the fun stuff. Amy is so bad and gets in so much trouble and never gets grounded." Kids may complain about your involvement, but they actually appreciate and need it. Do you watch your children and model proper behavior? Do you share your values and encourage them to follow? Do you leave your child unsupervised? Children do not really want to be unsupervised; they just think they do. Sports and activities were made for spectators, and who better than parents?

SECRET FOR SUCCESS #6: TEACH BASIC VALUES

When we build character and create nurturing family environments we provide children with a sense of community and purpose, as well as a strong foundation for a lifelong learning process.

One of the greatest gifts you can give your child is a strong sense of values, such as honesty and dependability. Teaching your children values is as important as teaching them how to read and provides the best protection from the negative influences that are all around them. Generally, private schools strongly emphasize values throughout the curriculum. Values must be instilled in every aspect of a child's life. Deciding whether something is right or wrong and acting on those feelings is an essential life skill. Values are learned from daily examples, and you are the one who sets the example.

Values have the power to guide children toward good choices. Family is the place where we learn what matters most. Do we teach kindness by the way we treat family members? Do we teach resourcefulness by the way we solve problems? The family unit is a classroom. Family members should share their best experiences and discuss the poor choices they made during the week and reflect why they were good or not so good and what could have been an alternate option.

The first step in teaching values to children is to decide what the most important values you hold and wish to instill into your children are. The second step involves creating a home life filled with love, kindness, and respect. The third step is to discuss and model one's values. And the fourth step is to empower children to make decisions and deal with consequences, both good and bad. Children need to understand that every choice they make has consequences and affects their lives.

When I think of values, this is what comes to mind: Values are instilled; they are learned and must be taught. What does instilled mean to you? I believe that instilled means something that is learned and carried out by following an example. You have to ask yourself as a parent, "How do I transmit values to my children?" I have to reflect back to my life, what my parents taught me, and the examples they gave me. Ask yourself, "What was it that gave me the values that I have as an adult?" Usually, the values that you have as an adult are those that were instilled in you as a child. So what are they? What are they and which ones do you want to relay to your children? Then, by example, you have to live by those values and act them out in everyday life. Discuss events that happened in your child's day. I know your children come home from school and say, "So and so did this," or "This one is in trouble for that," or "My friend was grounded." Use these comments as tools for discussing why the other child got in "trouble." Ask them, "Why do you think that person is grounded?" What did he do wrong? Then be prepared to discuss your child's response. For example, if she says, "He really didn't do anything; he just got caught cheating on a test. He was cheating because he didn't have time to study because his family had something to do after school," this is the time when a parent has to step in and say, "Let's talk about this a little more." A person who didn't have time to study has two choices. He may talk to his teacher and tell her what happened and ask for an extension, or he can just do the best he can, but he should never resort to cheating. Truth is a value. Truth and honesty are values. So this scenario is going to create a great setting for you to instill several values in your child. So you sit down with your child and talk. Okay, Johnny, what your friend should have done is been honest with the teacher; he should have told the truth. He should have said, "Mrs. Carter, I want to tell you that I wasn't able to study for this test and I am not prepared. My mom had an emergency after school and I didn't get home until 9:00 P.M. Is there any way you can give me one more day?" The teacher has options to say, "No, you knew about it for weeks" or "I understand and I'm going to help you."

Understanding and patience are other values we need to instill. We must accept the consequences of our actions and the decisions of others. If the response from the teacher is no, then the child should try his or her best, and if the child fails it is with dignity. Which value do you want your child to choose? Do you want to say, "You know what, sometimes in life it's okay to try your best in a given situation even if you are not successful"? Do you teach them to hold their heads up high and do their best the next time? Cheating is never the right route. Cheating is not a characteristic of a person with values. Cheating is the wrong thing to do, and it is not a value you want to promote in your child. You may be asking, "Do I punish them?" All children need to experience consequences for their actions. The consequence does not always have to be a traditional form of punishment. When a parent just says, "You're grounded," there is usually no lesson learned to prevent similar incidents in the future. It may even send the message that you don't care that your child had a problem and that they didn't ask for help. The parents could say, "Listen, Johnny, I'm not going to punish you now because I understand you didn't know what to do in this situation. I'm going to explain to you what was wrong." The value that the parent should stress is that you don't need to cheat, you need to do your best; when there is a problem you must ask for help.

Asking for help and looking for the proper solutions are other values to instill in your children. Why did this child cheat? Why did he choose to cheat and why would another person go to the teacher or go to a parent and ask for help? It's because the right values have not yet been instilled in this child. He's learned by example that if you can't do something, if you're not prepared, look for a shortcut. Look for the easy way to get the right results. That is incorrect. That is learned somewhere in the home. You have to watch the examples you give your children. You have to do the right thing, and, as a parent, you have to always remember that some little eyes and little ears are watching and listening and you have to make the right decisions. It starts with something as simple as driving through a yellow light. What does that show your child? Driving through a yellow light means I do not have the patience to sit here; I'm going to take a risk. This is what it means when you say "instill" the values in your children. They watch you and they listen to you all the time.

When you instill values in your child, these values will be reflected in your child's attitude toward school. If you show your child that you value school and learning, she will bring this attitude with her when she enters school. Your child will understand—again, if you instill this in her—that she is there to learn. Even though everyone else has to go to school, too, this is an opportunity that you are providing. You give children the tools and the resources to do well and learn and make a future for themselves, and they need to understand this. If you instill respect in them, they will respect their teachers; they will respect the idea of homework, projects, deadlines, and goals. They will be able to come to you, ask for help, and realize their full potential. At the same time, from young children up through the high school years, they will learn to respect each other and their elders. They'll learn to form relationships with respect, and they will learn to respect themselves. As they grow and as they change from children to young adults, respect is a very important part of what is going on with them, academically and socially.

At some point in this, pride sets in too. Pride in who they are, and the names that they carry should be evident in the papers that they turn in, in the test grades that they make, in the relationships that they establish, in their school, in the teams that they represent. These are all values that are learned. Yes, one child can be on the track team and give it his all. He will make sure to get adequate sleep the night before and eat a good breakfast. He will ask himself, "Am I ready to give this my best, make myself proud, make my family proud, make my school proud?" Then, another child will not care. He will stay up all night listening to music, have water and bagel for breakfast, and not give his all. Which is your child?

When your child is in a group or on a team, does she know her part and its importance? Does he understand that as a member of a team, you respect each other, and you give it your all for the team because your little part makes or breaks the result? Cooperation is vital both on the playing field and in life.

Pride is a value that will come out in your child's performance both in and outside the classroom. You must give all these tools to your children; it will be shown in who they are, how they represent you, how they represent their school, and their work.

GAINING THE PRIVATE SCHOOL EDGE: PRACTICAL TIPS, EXAMPLES, AND GUIDES TO GET YOU STARTED

Tip #1: Tell your children you love them . . . then tell them again. Do acts of kindness as a family. Discuss the concept of mutual respect.

Brittney, Age 11

Brittney is listening to the radio on her way home from school, and a car cuts off her mother. Her mother curses under her breath and makes a hand gesture out the window. Brittney's mother than races up to pass the car and cut it off.

Advice for Getting Brittney on the Right Track

Brittney's parents need reminding that they are their child's first teacher and how they respond and react is often how their daughter will respond and react. When encountering someone who is acting inappropriately or just plain getting on their nerves, they must explain how essential it is to obey rules and to react safely and kindly.

Your Current Situation: Where Are You Now?

Ask yourself these questions and reflect on the answers:

- When was the last time I did something I would not want my child to do?
- Do I discuss my basic values?
- Do I discuss better options when my child behaves inappropriately?
- Do I show my child that rules are to be followed?
- Do I treat others as I would like to be treated?

Tip #2: Allow children to make decisions and discuss the consequences, both good and bad. Practice what you preach.

Carlos, Age 8

Carlos comes home upset everyday because he is always missing things from his desk. His favorite markers, paper, and his big eraser are gone. One afternoon he arrives home and tells his mom not to worry, he solved his missing supplies problem. Carlos started taking things from other kids' desks to replace his missing stuff.

Advice for Getting Carlos on the Right Track

Stealing is never the right thing to do. Carlos's parents need to sit down and explain that even though someone is stealing from him, two wrongs do not make a right. They could advise him to notify the teacher of the constantly missing items from his desk. He could also place all his supplies in a bag and place them out of easy reach or temptation. Values must remain consistent in all circumstances.

Saying please and thank you and refraining from negative comments when encountering delays or difficult people show your child how to react in a difficult situation. Carrying out your responsibilities regardless of what is happening around you shows the importance of dedication and following through with tasks. Taking pride in all you do shows children that you must always try your best and put your best foot forward. Aristotle said, "We are what we repeatedly do. Excellence, then, is not an act, but a habit."

Describe the current practice in your home.

Example: When my child misbehaves, he is punished. His actions and other alternatives are never discussed.

_____
_____
_____
_____

Your Expectations: The ideal situation.

List the values you wish to instill in your children.

_____
_____
_____

Reaching the Goal: Discuss your values and instill those you want in your children.

Making It a Priority: Make it part of your daily routine to look for opportunities to model your values—in the grocery store, at a restaurant, or anywhere you can model values.

CHAPTER 7

You Make the Difference

> Parents who know their children's teachers and help with the homework
> and teach their kids right from wrong—these parents can make all the
> difference.
>
> —President Bill Clinton, State of the Union Address

Parenting is the greatest and most challenging job you will ever have.
There is no training manual and very little room for error. However,
there are certainties about parenting that may help make the parenting
journey easier and produce healthy and confident children. This book
has given you six secrets to assist in doing your most important work.

Most important is to remember that kids learn in homes that learn,
from parents who value learning. Parents should sit down with their kids
and talk about what the kids have learned in school and what they plan
to achieve. Parents should be familiar with school policies and stay informed on their childrens' progress. Don't wait for teachers to contact
you; take the initiative. Families who stay informed about their children's progress at school have higher-achieving children. Get involved
whenever possible. If you are not able to go into school and volunteer,
become involved at home. Read a story together with your children and
ask them about their school day and homework. Limit their television
viewing and initiate regular communication with your children. Send a
clear message that learning and schoolwork are important.

Talking with your children is one of the most critical steps to healthy
parenting. Young children begin life fascinated by language and communication. To the small child, a mother or father's words are important,

comforting, and soothing. Use this to your advantage. Start intimate communication early on about everything and you have a greater chance for continuing this communication into the teen years.

Communicating thoughts and ideas is not a skill you are born with. We often assume that our children know how to express themselves. The art of expression must be learned. Parents must give kids ways to talk about how they feel. Let your children know how important they are and that you want to hear what they have to say. Honesty and openness must be commended. Include your children in family discussions when appropriate. When talking is part of the daily routine, it becomes easier to deal with difficult subjects.

Children model the behavior of parents. How you express and handle yourself will usually determine how your children will as well. Speaking honestly and clearly, responding calmly, and listening carefully will occur only if children are provided with models and opportunities to practice. Kids need to learn to share more than just their belongings. They need to feel comfortable sharing their feelings, thoughts, and ideas.

I would like to share 10 simple rules you can use to open the lines of communication with your children and have them listening and telling you more.

RULE #1: LISTEN! LISTEN! LISTEN!

When they want to talk, stop everything. If you continue what you were doing they will "know" you don't care and do not have time for them. Avoid jumping in and not letting them vent or discuss their concerns, worries, and fears. In life, sometimes we all need a shoulder to cry on. At times, we don't even want advice or comments. Other times, we just want to be heard and feel like someone shares our pain. A silent and sympathetic ear is sometimes the best thing we can give to our children.

Here are a few words to show we are listening:

- Tell me more!
- I know.
- Wow!
- That is just awful.

- I am here.
- Go ahead, let it out.

RULE #2: THERE IS POWER IN CHOICE

When you are talking to your children, give them a choice whenever possible. Allow them to feel you are talking with them and asking them rather than talking at them or telling them. Make conversations a two-way street rather than a power struggle.

RULE #3: AVOID UNTRUE STATEMENTS AND THINGS SAID OUT OF ANGER AND FRUSTRATION

Your children will learn to listen and believe when you speak to them truthfully and calmly. Trust and respect comes from honesty and sincerity. If you do not mean it, don't say it.

RULE #4: BE A SOURCE OF ENCOURAGEMENT

When your children confides in you, they should feel relieved, inspired, and recharged rather than guilty or that they are a source of disappointment to you. When they come to you with a problem or situation, offer your ear as well as words of encouragement.

The following are examples of words of encouragement:

- I know you can handle it.
- Every problem has a solution, even this.
- Think it over, you will figure this out.
- I am here to help you.
- I went through this at your age, like when . . .

RULE # 5: MAKE YOUR CONVERSATIONS A PLACE OF COMFORT

Try to step away from being the parent when listening and put yourself in your child's shoes. Think about how difficult the conversation may be for him or her and think before you react.

RULE # 6: AVOID THE TWENTY QUESTIONS OR DRILL ROUTINE

Try not to take over the conversation. If they share something with you and feel like they are being scolded or feel like they are disappointing you, they will probably not let it happen again. As a parent, there will be times when you must address an issue they discuss with you; be sure you address the behavior or action and not the child.

RULE # 7: MAKE A POINT OF BEING THE INITIATOR

Out of the blue, follow up on a previous subject of interest before they come to you. This reinforces your concern, as well as bringing you into their circle.

RULE # 8: TAKE TIME TO SHARE

A busy parent is not always the best parent. Drop everything and do something spontaneous like taking in a movie on a school day or doing homework in the park.

RULE # 9: APOLOGIZE WHEN YOU ARE WRONG

If you say something or do something you probably shouldn't have, say you are sorry. Admit you are human too and make mistakes.

RULE #10: LOVE THEM!

Don't just love them . . . tell them you love them. Show them the affection just as you did when they were small. Bake a cake for no occasion, play a game, take a walk after dinner. Show your love by showing them there is no better time than time spent with them.

In reading this book, I hope you gained some insights into how you can help your child become a successful student and an excited learner. All parents should take time to reflect on the things they do or don't do with their children and make some changes for the better. Remember, nothing happens overnight. Start setting goals for your children and working toward them and never give up. These six secrets discussed a lot you may have already known and just needed reminding. It's time to get started and know that nothing worthwhile is ever easy, but boy, there is something to celebrate in the end.

As a resident of south Florida, I have tried to forget the hurricane season of 2004, but from every "bad" thing usually comes a good lesson or revelation. This hurricane season gave me a couple of reminders I must share. Everything that we do for our children and everything we want for our children is extremely important, but all of our efforts are wasted without one essential ingredient, and that is love. Spending a couple of days in a dark shuttered home, sometimes just by candlelight, I had almost 72 hours of time just laying in bed and snuggling on the couch with my two sons. This time reminded me that as I read with them every day, practice their multiplication tables, and set goals and expectations, I must incorporate love into the equation. In searching for their weaknesses and helping them overcome them, we, as parents, must remind them of how proud we are of them and their efforts. None of our assistance is beneficial without reminding them every day that they are the most important things in the world and that we love them no matter what.

During the storms, my family and I were amazed how much fun we could have together without television, cable, or electric just by going back to old-fashioned board games, looking through some photo albums, and just telling stories. We had forgotten how much fun it can be just to sit in the dark and talk. Our children grow up fast, way, way too fast, and it's important that in all the rushing around, in getting them to study and do their homework, and to get adequate sleep and rest and having them do independent reading and a lot of the other things that I've mentioned in this book, that we also take time to stop and smell the roses. We should enjoy our children every day as we teach them to enjoy the world around them.

We want happy students, and that's what we have to think about every day, in every action that we take with our children, and especially when we're talking about school. Learning should be fun. Children thrive when they are having fun, because after all, who wouldn't choose something that's fun? Learning and achieving should make us feel good. When we feel good, we want to do good, and when we do good, we feel good, and that's a wonderful cycle that we want to promote in our kids.

Remember though, that showing love to your children is not always hugs and kisses. Sometimes the greatest love is discipline. "No, you're not going out with your friend; you need to clean up your room." "I'm sorry, but you can't have anyone over today because it's a school night." "The television needs to be turned off. You had your 30 minutes today and now it's time to take out a book or get a good night's rest." Love your children. Love them with all of the passion that you have inside you, but remember, it's okay to say no. In fact, children expect it. Of course they are going to pout and be annoyed, but never forget, mommy knows best, daddy knows best, and you know best, and your children one day will realize this, too. So show them you love them by telling them no and surprising them with yes, giving them ground rules and making them carry them out. Expect their best. Take an interest in everything that they do because nothing goes farther than an interested parent. Believe me, children are smarter and smarter every single year, and they know when you're interested and they know when you're not. They know when you're listening and they know when you're not. They know when you care and they know when you don't. They know when you're serious and they know when you're not. Make sure every day you set the example for learning because it can be contagious.

Show your children the wonderful world around them and that there is a never-ending possibility for discovery. We want curious children. We want excited children. We want responsible children. We want children to grow up to be responsible decision makers, and the parents' job is to help them with those problem-solving skills. Regardless of your child's school, none of this happens without a supporting, loving parent. And that's you!

Parenting takes reflection skills—looking back and deciding things we're going to try not to do again and things we're going to try in the future. Make a vision for your child and help him or her every single day. Don't forget every once in a while to just grab them, put them under the blanket with you, and tell them, "You can be anything and I believe in you." Remember that sometimes, no matter how hard we try, children will resist, and as they grow forcing usually does not work. As active parents, you need to inspire them and never give up. You know what you want; you decide what you expect from them and then help them along the way. Remember, sometimes it is uphill.

There are many different strategies that can be used to incorporate my six simple secrets into your life. All children are different and all parents are different. You need to use the strategy that best suits your lifestyle and your child's needs.

If you think back to your own education you probably remember subjects that you studied about which you remember a lot of the facts and information you learned. Then you have others where the material is vaguely recognizable to you. The encouragement and the excitement about learning are what really make children gain valuable information and a strong foundation to help them throughout their lives and in higher education. Make sure, as your children are learning and studying, that it's not just for an exam or a test or a grade, but it's to gain valuable information.

You can ensure they remember most of what they learn. You can do this by asking them every day, "What did you learn? What was the most interesting thing? What should we share with your brother or sister? What should we share with grandma or grandpa? What else can we learn about that?" This allows children to relate information to new things they'll learn and to be excited to learn more. We don't want children to memorize things, to take a test at school and have the information disappear 5 minutes after the test. We want to inspire them to want to know more and more.

This book has really talked about six secrets to help your child succeed in school. Before I can feel comfortable leaving you, I have to say that all of the advice I have given you for your children about eating nutritious meals, not being overscheduled, and getting enough rest is just as necessary for you. As the sign in my grandmother's house said, "If mamma's happy, everybody's happy." It's important for all parents to take time for themselves. Adults need downtime as well—time to rest, time to do nothing. Go have a manicure, a pedicure, a happy hour or movie once in a while. Yes, we are the first teachers of our children, and yes, we are extremely important, but we're also individuals who need time away. I want you to inspire learning in your children. I want you to teach them something every day. I want you to be their cheer-leader. I want you to be their disciplinarian, but it can't be 24/7. Everything needs to be in moderation and balance, and as parents, if we're not happy, rested adults, we can't be the type of moms and dads that our children need to achieve. If we want children who are happy, successful students, we have to be happy adults. Get started today; follow these secrets and you can and will raise successful children, in and out of the classroom.

References

Clinton, William J. (1994, January 25). Address before a joint session of the Congress on the State of the Union. In *Public Papers of the Presidents, Volume 1* (pp. 126–135). Washington, DC: U.S. Government Printing Office.

Johnston, L. D., O'Malley, P. M., Bachman, J. G., & Schulenberg, J. E. (2004). *Monitoring the future: National survey results on drug use, 1975–2003. Volume I: Secondary school students* (NIH Publication No. 04-5507). Bethesda, MD: National Institute on Drug Abuse.

National Center for Chronic Disease Prevention and Health Promotion. (2001). *Youth Risk Behavior Survey*. Washington, DC: U.S. Government Printing Office.

About the Author

Meline M. Kevorkian, Ed.D., is an assistant principal in southern Florida, adjunct professor at Nova Southeastern University, and a columnist with the *Miami Herald*. She has practical experience in both public and private schools from preschool to the university level.